THE ANUNNAKI TAROT

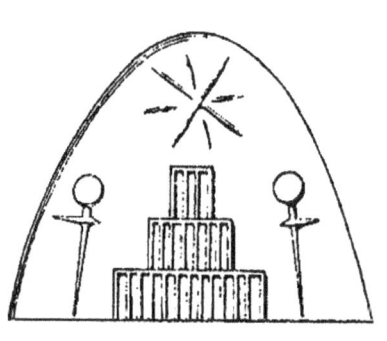

FIRST EDITION

THE ANUNNAKI TAROT

Consulting the Babylonian Oracle of Cosmic Wisdom

Designed by Joshua Free
Graphics by Kyra Kaos

PUBLISHED BY THE **JOSHUA FREE** IMPRINT REPRESENTING
Mardukite Truth Seeker Press — mardukite.com

© 2019, JOSHUA FREE & KYRA KAOS

ISBN : 978-0-578-46843-3

No part of this publication may be reproduced in any form or by any means, electronic or mechanical, including photocopying, recording, or any information storage or retrieval system, without permission in writing from the publisher.

Originally published to compliment—
 ANUNNAKI TAROT:
   THE BABYLONIAN ORACLE OF
   COSMIC WISDOM (CARDS)
   Created by Joshua Free & Kyra Kaos

Tablet Extracts and Quotations derived from—
 THE COMPLETE ANUNNAKI BIBLE
     (edited by Joshua Free)
 THE SUMERIAN LEGACY (by Joshua Free)

TABLET OF CONTENTS
— —

Introduction . . . 7

THE CARDS
  Card Description Key . . . 13
  0. Adamu . . . 17
  1. Marduk . . . 21
  2. Teshmet . . . 25
  3. Sarpanit . . . 29
  4. Anu . . . 33
  5. Nabu . . . 37
  6. Divine Union . . . 41
  7. Winged Disc . . . 45
  8. Elder Sign . . . 49
  9. E.A.-Enki . . . 53
  10. Tablet of Destiny . . . 57
  11. Enlil . . . 61
  12. Marduk's Exile . . . 65
  13. The Cosmic Tree . . . 69
  14. The Path . . . 73
  15. Tiamat . . . 77
  16. Marduk's Temple . . . 81
  17. Inanna–Ishtar . . . 85
  18. Nanna–Sin . . . 89

19. Shammash (Šamaš) ... 93
20. Anunnaki Assembly ... 97
21. An-Ki ... 101

THE ORACLE
  Consulting the Oracle ... 107
  The Card Spreads ... 114
  Babili – Gates of Babylon ... 115
  Etemenanki – Tower of Babylon ... 117
  Esagila – Temple of Marduk ... 119
  Anunna – Anunnaki Assembly ... 122
  Istari – The Anunnaki Star ... 126

APPENDIX
  Anunnaki Tarot Paper Deck ... 132

INTRODUCTION
— —

Of nearly 25 years actively involved with the modern "New Age" or "metaphysical" revival, I have now spent over ten of them as Director of the "Mardukite Research Organization." All during this time I collected notes for a guidebook, hoping I would one day be partnered with a graphic artist that could both appreciate efforts to bring my *Anunnaki Tarot* to light and be able to enhance ancient specimens of Mesopotamian art that fit my specification—rather than apply modern art to ancient archetypes.

Ancient archetypes of civilization actually originate in Mesopotamia—so, rather than take an arbitrary theme and impose tarot symbolism onto it, my esoteric knowledge base of Anunnaki traditions allowed me to quite easily bridge these two aspects in a way both historically authentic and mystically valid as a practical tool of modern "Mardukite neo-Babylonian spirituality."

This is not the first time that Mesopotamia makes an appearance in tarot—however, it is the first time that the post-Sumerian or "Mardukite" Babylonian paradigm/worldview is represented properly. Where some have presented what they call Babylonian, in reality we are given combinations of the Babylonian and pre-Mardukite or Enlilite systems interchangeably and often placing emphasis on deities and myths that aren't central to Mardukite Babylonian religion.

I selected the title *Anunnaki Tarot* for this oracle to differentiate from other artistic manifestations of a Babylonian tarot that previously emphasized Sumerian motifs or the "Epic of Gilgamesh" but not Mardukite Babylon as reflected in a tablet catalogue the Mardukite Research Organization prepared as "The Complete Anunnaki Bible." The specifically Mardukite tablets display a mystical tradition of Babylon under the patron Anunnaki deity Marduk, whose son Nabu established the tradition with a proliferation of cuneiform tablets supporting the systematization of Anunnaki tradition.

Our *Anunnaki Tarot* guidebook does not replace a knowledge-base in Mesopotamian lore, history and geography—like those I have prepared elsewhere in previous texts such as *The Complete Anunnaki Bible: Source Book of Esoteric Archaeology*, or *The Sumerian Legacy: Guide to Esoteric Archaeology*. What this book does is concisely align the tarot symbolism with a comprehensive review of Anunnaki archetypes as they appear in Ancient Babylonian Mardukite tradition.

This project has been a constant work of devotion. Any intended use or deeper potential of this system is self-evident for those studying previous "Mardukite" materials or those interested in Mesopotamia and its modern spiritual revivals. It is curious to see how far the Anunnaki paradigm has come in just ten years. It will be interesting to see how this tarot reinvigoration will be received. I hope you enjoy!

> JOSHUA FREE, "NABU"
> New Babylon Research Office
> Akiti/Akitu – March 21, 2019

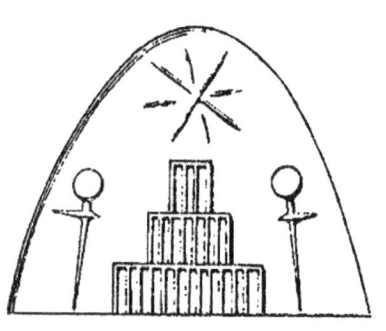

THE CARDS

CARD DESCRIPTION KEY

"Names and Titles."
"Tablet Quote"
[Background Information]

ESOTERIC CORRESPONDENCE.

Card Number : Numeric designation based on traditional tarot arrangements.

Babylonian Anunnaki or *Archetype* : A name or example of the Anunnaki deity or Mesopotamian archetype as best known in "Mardukite" Babylonian or neo-Babylonian tradition.

Sumerian Anunnaki or *Archetype* : A name or example of the Anunnaki deity or Mesopotamian archetype as best known in Enlilite, pre-Babylonian or "Old Sumerian" tradition.

Mesopotamian Numerology : Esoteric numeric designation based on Babylonian sexagesimal correspondences from Mesopotamian lore.

Tarot Equivalent : The traditional tarot key or card from the standard Major or Greater Arcana represented.

Runic Symbolism : For divinatory purposes- the corresponding (Nordic) Rune Key with similar interpretation.

Ogham Symbolism : For divinatory purposes- the corresponding (Celtic) Ogham Key with similar interpretation.

Kabbalistic : An association of tarot keys for plotting along the "paths" of the (Hebrew) Kabbalah, which was first based on Babylonian lore.

Astrological : An association of celestial keys plotting energies from the planets and zodiac stars (Celestial Sphere) for an astrological description.

Cosmic System Domain : Major systems and fixed systems related to Cosmic Law that are best represented.

Arts of Civilization : The Divine "ME" or Arts (systems) of Civilization, Divine Decrees and Divine Objects that are best represented.

Keyword : A basic fundamental concept or idea that best gives an overview.

DIVINATION SYMBOLISM.

Description : A graphic description of the visual imagery specifically selected to represent within this tarot.

Meaning : A comprehensive list of factors, states or aspects represented by the card key. These traditional concepts are derived from both Mesopotamian lore and classic icons within tarot use. These ideas may be attracted by meditation, talismanic use of imagery or used as a "significator" when querying.

Personality : When used to indicate specific persons, known or unknown, this key may be consulted (as replacing use of "court" cards) for this pack.

Reversed : Alternate meanings associated with inversion or the opposite pole of a spectrum. Use of talismans or in meditation: these traits may be turned or polarized to attract the more desired aspect of the energy.

0. ADAMU
"Primitive Man"

*"Flesh and blood of the god was mixed with
clay to house the spirit.
To the Adamu they sought to bestow the
face of the gods."*
*"And Enki did procreate with an Adamu
female on Earth.
Enki gave to him a wide ear,
granting him wisdom."*
"Enki had created him to be chief of men."
—Mardukite Tablet-G

Cuneiform tablets describe the Anunnaki as the "creators of humanity," upgrading their genetics, intelligence, social systems and installing themselves as a pantheon of gods among the most ancient urbanized institutions. In some interpretations, the upgraded humans were a "slave race" for the gods, performing manual labor of digging canals, building structures, making clay bricks, producing food—all of which are among the god's "gifts" to humanity.

The "adamu" race represented a fresh new set of possibilities for evolution on earth. When the Anunnaki god Enki decided to upgrade the race further, granting Adapa the wisdom of the gods, these possibilities became literally astronomical—evolution that might have otherwise taken millions of years was reached overnight. This new birth is only potential. Developments are yet to be determined as a "new initiate" is first set upon the path—as an individual—to travel up the ladder of lights, ascending to unite with the highest mystic spiritual oneness we were birthed from.

ESOTERIC CORRESPONDENCE.

Card Number : 0
Babylonian Archetype : Adapa ("wisest among men")
Sumerian Archetype : A-da-mu; Lu.Lu ("primitive worker")
Tarot Equivalent : The Fool.
Runic Symbolism : Mannaz
Ogham Symbolism : Heather ("ur")
Kabbalistic : Crown of Wisdom.

Astrological : "Primary Action" through the Air element on the zodiac.
Cosmic System (Domain) : Virtue of Faith.
Arts of Civilization (MEs) : Heroship
Keywords : Man-child of Earth.

DIVINATION SYMBOLISM.

Description : The Anunnaki mother goddess is seated with the newly birthed upgraded human being on her lap.

Meaning : Beginnings (of a journey, project or major cycle), a crossroads, clean slate, potential and possibilities, important decisions and choices, wisdom is required, looking to the past (experiences and mistakes) before acting.

Personality : An innocent or young person; a new person enters the situation.

Reversed : Uncertainty and insecurity, unclear or unsure actions, failure to act or take first steps, a need to listen to the "voice of the Self."

1. MARDUK
"Master of Magicians"

*"Marduk passed through and surveyed
the regions of Heaven
and fixed the star gates of the Elder Gods."*
*"I bind the Elder Gods to the Watchtowers,
says Marduk,
I bind the Watcher to the Gate,
with the key known only to my race."*
—Mardukite Tablet-N

In the post-Sumerian Mardukite Babylon, Marduk is placed at the height of the pantheon—a representation of the raw and industrious power of *Jupiter*—a position held by Enlil in the original mythology. A prowess in magic elevated Marduk in the pantheon—as described on the Babylonian Tablets of Creation, the *Enuma Elis*, earning him also the title: "Master of Magicians." This craft of magic—or esoteric sciences—was learned from an apprenticeship in the first city on earth, *Eridu*, home to the Anunnaki god Enki, the Father of Marduk.

Marduk demonstrates an application of supreme "will" and an understanding of the ordering in the cosmos to execute his preparations and systematization of the "cosmic gates" in alignment with "cosmic law." This practice toward a higher use of will and pursuit of higher knowledge has ever after defined the magical arts.

ESOTERIC CORRESPONDENCE.

Card Number : 1
Babylonian Anunnaki : Marduk, Mar.Dug, Merodak
Sumerian Anunnaki : A.Mar.Utu or Amar-utuk, Asar.Luli, Asari-lu-du
Mesopotamian Numerology : 10 (also 6 and 50)
Tarot Equivalent : The Magician.
Ogham Symbolism : Mistletoe
Kabbalistic : Crown of Understanding.
Astrological : "Primary Substance" acting through Mercury on Saturn.
Cosmic Domain : Sphere/Gate of Jupiter.
Divine Object (MEs) : Exalted wand-sceptre.
Keyword : Use of Will.

DIVINATION SYMBOLISM.

Description : Marduk stands wearing the holy regalia and tablets of power around his neck standing next to the "sirrush" dragon of Babylon, a power symbol for the legacy of Mardukite gods Marduk and Nabu.

Meaning : Application of will and abilities, moving forward (right direction), use of knowledge for creativity (manifestation); using talent, skill, ability, dexterity to productive ends; innovation and ceremonial (magical) arts.

Personality : A skilled, talented, intelligent person; an emerging strong talent.

Reversed : Abuse of will/power and selfish use of manipulation (destructive ends); inability to adopt or cope; inability to learn from experience; confusion and uncoordinated or unbalanced actions.

2. TESHMET
"The High Priestess"

"O Lady Tasmitu, listen to the Incantation!
Before Nabu, thy spouse, the lord, the prince,
the firstborn of the E.Sag.Ila,
intercede for me!
May he hearken to my cry...
May he learn of my supplication..."
—The Sumerian Legacy

Teshmet—or Tasmitu—as consort of Nabu, is the definitive High Priestess of the post-Sumerian "Mardukite" paradigm. Where Nabu is the divine herald and projector of communication, Teshmet is the goddess of reception, goddess of hearing—listener of the prayers and supplications, acting as an intermediary between the people and the Anunnaki offices of godhood. Teshmet and Nabu are both earthborn, descended from the "Sky God" pantheon, but most closely connected to the earth planet: its systems and inhabitants. Thus, "priesthoods" were born as intermediary civic institutions.

Sumerian priestesses were first dedicated to Inanna-Ishtar, as is also evident among early practices of the lunar-cult of Nanna. In Babylon, the practices shift from more physical primitive rites toward those more intellectually and spiritually oriented with prayers and meditation.

ESOTERIC CORRESPONDENCE.

Card Number : 2
Babylonian Anunnaki : Tas.Mit, Tasmitu, Teshmet, Teshmetum ("Listener")
Sumerian Anunnaki : Ur-me-tum
Tarot Equivalent : The High Priestess.
Runic Symbolism : Uruz
Ogham Symbolism : Hazel ("coll")
Kabbalistic : Wisdom of Understanding.
Astrological : "Primary Motion" acting through the Moon onto the Sun.
Cosmic System (Domain) : Sphere of Mercury (consort to Nabu); Goddess of Supplication.
Arts of Civilization (MEs) : Priestesshood.
Divine Object (MEs) : The Cult Chamber.
Keyword : Hearer of Prayers.

DIVINATION SYMBOLISM.

Description : The bust of a statue of Teshmet as priestess and consort of Nabu in Borsippa, with hands clasped in a gesture-sign of priests and scribes of Mardukite Babylon.

Meaning : Intuitive awareness, listening (learning) and understanding (knowing); spiritual inspiration and connectedness (spiritual ideals and pursuits); divination (divining secrets), uncovering secrets/ hidden influences (that may prove beneficial).

Personality : A virtuous scholarly woman; a female "wise beyond her years" or feminine "old soul."

Reversed : Ignorance or naivete; requires self-honesty, suppression of feelings, superficial situations, lack of clarity and lack of secrets.

3. SARPANIT
"Queen of Babylon"

*"Sarpanit, Queen of the E.Sag.Ila,
Lady of Babylon, shadow over the lands,
Lady of the gods, who loves to give life,
Who protect life,
who gives offspring and seed,
who has made the people,
the whole of creation."*
—The Sumerian Legacy

Sarpanit, as the consort of Marduk, is elevated to the position of Queen in Babylon. She is an earthborn goddess, seventh generation descendent of (Enki's) Adapa, and the mother of Nabu. This position in combination with her relationship-role with Marduk also reflects in her elevation as a "Mother Goddess" in Mardukite tradition, where she also carries a former Sumerian title—Erua—"Mother of Seeds." Marduk's decision to marry Sarpanit—as opposed to Inanna-Ishtar—cost him rights of heaven: so he chose to rule on earth…in Babylon.

As a mystic symbol, the mother goddess or queen may represent physical fertility in the way of pregnancy and motherhood, but it more strongly embodies the spirit of "nurturing," a quality of motherhood, also necessary for producing any results.

ESOTERIC CORRESPONDENCE.

Card Number : 3
Babylonian Anunnaki : Sarpanit, Zarpanitu, Sarapan
Sumerian Anunnaki : Eru or Erua ("mother of seeds")
Mesopotamian Numerology : 5 (or 45 as the consort of Marduk's elevated 50)
Tarot Equivalent : The Empress.
Runic Symbolism : Berkana
Ogham Symbolism : Apple ("quert")
Kabbalistic : Crown of Beauty
Astrological : Celestial Sphere acting through Venus on Saturn.
Cosmic System (Domain) : Sphere of Moon & Venus (in Mardukite tradition)
Arts of Civilization (MEs) : Lasting Ladyship.
Keyword : Mother Goddess.

DIVINATION SYMBOLISM.

Description : The goddess Sarpanit stands in starry robes as consort of Marduk, elevated in status for Babylon and nearly equal in esteem to Inanna-Ishtar for the Mardukite tradition.

Meaning : Material/maternal growth and fertility, prosperity (abundance), satisfactory progress (needs being met), planting seeds (of longevity); results as wonderful harvest or new birth (pregnancy) marriage or motherhood.

Personality : A strong (or lavish) female; a maternal figure (mother) or handmaiden.

Reversed : Decadence (wasteful of resources), Poverty or the inability to meet satisfactory requirements (or obligations), emptiness (sterility, barren), withdrawal, domestic instability; infidelity or widowed.

4. ANU
"Heavenly King"

"Anu, King in Heaven,
Eternal Prince of the Anunnaki,
Whose words are the rule over
the Anunnaki Assembly.
The ears of the Igigi are directed
to hear your pure words.
May all the gods of heaven and earth
pray at your altar of offering."
—Mardukite Tablet-P

Anu is named for his role as the "Father in Heaven," the All-Father and supreme King of the Anunnaki gods. In the pantheon he is the father of both Enki and Enlil, each a head of their own lineage of deities, each a prince of their own domain in the cosmos. But, it is Anu who is a father and director to them all, though distant from the direct affairs of worldly interest. As such, his All-as-One heavenly force is not necessarily felt as present in obvious ways—the more visible aspects being left to his delegates.

Astrologically, the "House of Anu" is the "Throne of Heaven" or the planet Uranus. Its unique 84-year orbit, with four 21-year quarter turns, seems to share an affinity with the generational cycles of human life on earth. As each turn is a set of 7-year cycles, there is also a resonance to phases of human cellular regeneration as well.

ESOTERIC CORRESPONDENCE.

Card Number : 4
Babylonian Anunnaki : Anu
Sumerian Anunnaki : An
Mesopotamian Numerology : 60
Tarot Equivalent : The Emperor.
Runic Symbolism : Thurisa
Ogham Symbolism : Oak ("duir")
Kabbalistic : Wisdom of Beauty.
Astrological : Celestial Sphere acting
     through Aries on the Sun.
Cosmic Domain : Sphere/Gate of Uranus.
Arts of Civilization (MEs) : Anuship (Godhead),
     Kingship.
Divine Object (MEs) : The Enduring Crown.
Keyword : The All-Father of Heaven.

DIVINATION SYMBOLISM.

Description : A statue of Anu, the strong and mighty heavenly king with divine objects of royal regalia.

Meaning : External / material / worldly authority; the application of leadership for achievements and accomplishment; balanced self-management; responsible use (or delegation) of power/authority; striving for personal or business success.

Personality : A strong (ambitious) leader; a strong (accomplished) male figure.

Reversed : Incompetent leadership, lack of self-control, overwhelmed with responsibility, showing weakness, requiring self-discipline; motives questionable (self or others); the idea of doing something "no matter the costs."

5. NABU
"The High Priest-Scribe"

"Nabu, Royal Son of Marduk and Sarpanit,
Given the secrets of writing and wisdom,
The messenger [herald] of Marduk,
And organizer of the Mardukite Tribes,
Counselor to the scribes and prophets
of Marduk in Borsippa and Babylon..."
—Mardukite Tablet-A

Systematized or cataloged knowledge and wisdom is strongly connected to the arts of divination—the relay of information out in the universe, or else, communication of knowledge and Cosmic Laws. This domain is specific to the "priesthood" in Babylon. Whether it is prayer, hymn songs, records of history and commerce or predictions of the future—the performance or conduct was undertaken by a priesthood of scribes and under the blessing of the patron deity of scribes, the "Divine Scribal-Messenger" named Nabu, the "Mardukite herald" and firstborn heir-son of Marduk and Sarpanit.

Nabu's priest-scribes of Babylon carried a responsibility of devising and maintaining the literary tablet collection in support of a new post-Sumerian "Babylonian" Anunnaki paradigm we refer to as "Mardukite," using the *Enuma Elis* and other tablets to elevate Marduk to the height of the pantheon.

ESOTERIC CORRESPONDENCE.

Card Number : 5
Babylonian Anunnaki : Nabu
Sumerian Anunnaki : En-sag, Tutu, Nisaba.
Mesopotamian Numerology : 12 (also 2)
Tarot Equivalent : The High Priest.
Runic Symbolism : Perth
Ogham Symbolism : Rowen ("luis")
Kabbalistic : Wisdom of Mercy.
Astrological : Celestial Sphere acting
 through Taurus on Jupiter.
Cosmic Domain : Sphere/Gate of Mercury.
Arts of Civilization (MEs) : "Scribeship"
 (Grammar, Logic, Rhetoric)
Keyword : The Divine Librarian.

DIVINATION SYMBOLISM.

Description : A statue of Nabu, high priest of Marduk, scribe-patron of Borsippa, with hands clasped in the gesture-sign of the Mardukite priesthood.

Meaning : Establishment, organization of knowledge (solid systematization); policy (bureaucracy), conformity (over originality), traditions, solidifying foundations by recognizing (pursuing) truth; spiritual (divine) inspiration (religion).

Personality : A nice intelligent person, but potentially stubborn/exasperating.

Reversed : Refusal to recognize objective truth; unorthodoxy, originality, creativity in solving problems; not afraid to venture forth (trailblazing) into uncharted terrain.

6. DIVINE UNION
"The Lovers"

"My high priest, says Inanna-Ishtar,
is ready for the holy loins.
My lord, Dumuzi, is ready for the holy loins.
The plants and herbs in his field are ripe.
Let the bed that rejoices the heart,
be prepared!
Let the bed of kingship be prepared!
Let the bed of queenship be prepared!"
—Mardukite Tablet-U

Gender equality appears in Mesopotamian culture and Anunnaki divinity more prominently, perhaps, than any other paradigm or worldview. Each quality or facet of the cosmos is represented by a combined form of male and female aspects—reflected in public exoteric religions, respectively, as a god and goddess, acting together as one to form active motion of one current-stream. This pendulous motion represents an ebb and flow, peak and valley, contraction and expansion of the same singular force.

Cuneiform tablets spare no details regarding the romantic exploits and courtships between Anunnaki deities. Divine Couplehood became a staple of the tradition and a model or representation of the highest "union" or "marriage" possible. (A few of these couples are listed below.) Marriage and legal rights to protect the women and their property were institutionalized with Hammurabi's Code.

ESOTERIC CORRESPONDENCE.

Card Number : 6
Babylonian Archetype : Marduk & Sarpanit; Nabu & Teshmet.
Sumerian Archetype : Nergal & Ereshkigal; Inanna-Ishtar & Tammuz-Dumuzi.
Tarot Equivalent : The Lovers.
Runic Symbolism : Gebo
Ogham Symbolism : Vine ("muin")
Kabbalistic : Understanding of Beauty.
Astrological : Saturn acting through Gemini on the Sun.
Cosmic System (Domain) : The Law of Polarity & Gender; Virtue of Love.

Arts of Civilization (MEs) : Sexual union, sexual intercourse.

Divine Decree (MEs) : "Hierodule of Heaven" ("Sacred Prostitution")

Keyword : Sacred Marriage (Hieros Gamos)

DIVINATION SYMBOLISM.

Description : An Anunnaki couple courts one another in the ritual of divine marriage beneath the cosmic tree.

Meaning : Partnerships and coupling; union or combination (unity of two or more 'parts'); counterparts and consorts (relationships), social choices (challenges and decisions); possibly indicating romantic love.

Personality : Two of something; a group; a couple; company or organization.

Reversed : Separations and fragmentation (division and breakups); conflicts (disagreement), tragic unions (couples divided); the temptation of betrayal.

7. WINGED DISC
"The Fiery Chariot"

"Marduk made ready the bow,
his first choice in weapons.
He slung a spear upon him.
He raised the club in his right hand.
The bow and the quiver he hung at his side.
He set the Flaming Disc in front of him,
and with the Flame, he filled his body."
—Mardukite Tablet-N

Often depicted in Mesopotamian art as an emblem of divinity, scholars interpret the winged disc in many ways, including the sun, a planet, a star, a supernova, a comet, some other kind of satellite—and even a spaceship. Whatever the nature of winged and flaming discs in the sky, it is at least clear that it represents action, energetic activity or *movement* in the cosmos or following Cosmic Law. One prominent use of the symbol in Babylon depicted Marduk as seated within a winged disc; an icon later called *Faravahar* by Persian Zoroastrians.

In ancient Egypt and Mesopotamia, winged discs or suns also served as insignias of royalty—representing the "highest"—or to things belonging to the gods or the kings. Later "Hermetic" magic schools included this image at the apex of a "sacred wand" or "serpent staff" (of Hermes, Thoth, Enki, Nabu or Ningishzida) representing authority, knowledge and power of Cosmic Law.

ESOTERIC CORRESPONDENCE.

Card Number : 7
Babylonian Archetype : Solar/Stellar Disc
Sumerian Archetype : The Visible Force
Mesopotamian Numerology : 360
Tarot Equivalent : The Chariot.
Runic Symbolism : Ehwaz
Ogham Symbolism : Holly ("tinne")
Kabbalistic : Understanding of Strength.
Astrological : Saturn acting through Cancer on Mars.
Cosmic System : The Law of Rhythm.
Arts of Civilization (MEs) : Chronology, Vibration, Music, Movement.
Keyword : Physical Action.

DIVINATION SYMBOLISM.

Description : A famous depiction of the winged solar/stellar or astral disc of divine power shining over earth.

Meaning : Movement (application and motion of energy), re-dedication (devotion) to the cause (faith); the self-discipline to see past obstacles (achieve victory, triumph); action and physical movement across space; travel (physical or astral), motion as the pendulum of forces/opposition.

Personality : Adventurer boldly seeking new ventures, experiences and places.

Reversed : Failure to execute plans (move energy properly); wasteful efforts (improper use of momentum or inertia); improper vibrations, failure to take considerations or concern of consequences (and the sequences of action).

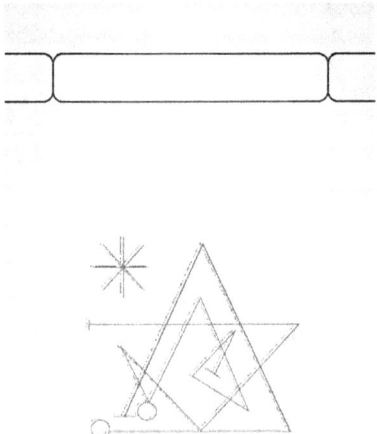

8. ELDER SIGN
"Strength of the Gods"

*"Collecting the powers of Anu, Enlil and Enki to himself,
Marduk passed through and surveyed the regions of heaven, establishing districts for Anu, Enlil and Enki to reign.
Enlil game to Marduk his name and title.
Enki gave to Marduk his name and title, saying, 'the binding of all my decrees, let Marduk now control.'"*
—Mardukite Tablet-F & N

The power and strength of the Anunnaki gods is always rooted in authority, divine right and Cosmic Law. In fact, even among the "younger generation" of Anunnaki, all esoteric, occult or otherwise cosmic reign was conducted in accordance with "names and numbers" of formulae specific to the "Supernal Trinity" of Anunnaki gods: Anu, Enlil and Enki. Tablets were formed by the priesthoods to show that elevation of one deity or another was divinely ordained.

The Elder Sign is considered a "glyph" or *sigil* representing total power/authority of the Anunnaki Supernal Trinity—as is used by Marduk to establish cosmic star gates. Later Babylonian interpretations may substitute identifying Trinity names, but the basic meaning remains unchanged.

ESOTERIC CORRESPONDENCE.

Card Number : 8
Babylonian Archetype : "Elder Sign" or mer-ka-ba.
Sumerian Archetype : ad-da dub-sar ("the father sigil")
Tarot Equivalent : Strength
Runic Symbolism : Wunjo
Ogham Symbolism : Alder ("fearn")
Kabbalistic : Mercy of Strength (Severity)
Astrological : Jupiter acting through Leo onto Mars.
Cosmic System : The Law of Analogy and Correspondence.
Arts of Civilization (MEs) : Virtue of Strength.
Divine Object (MEs) : Insignia of Divine Power.
Keyword : Protection and (Inner) Power.

DIVINATION SYMBOLISM.

Description : The supreme sigil or "Elder Sign" representing total cosmic power and the authority of the "Supernal Trinity"—Anu, Enlil and Enki; Anu, Enki and Marduk; Enki, Marduk and Nabu, &tc.

Meaning : Organization and consolidation of higher (inner) power (strength); divine power (protection), mental fortitude by conquering emotion, sealing reality (divine providence) with proper observation of Divine Law; longevity and endurance of Cosmic Law, Natural Law.

Personality : A confident individual; a fortuitous enduring person.

Reversed : Weakness (disorganization), Defeat or surrender (succumbing to pressures from above/outside); false strength (empty dominance) and failure to maintain integrity.

9. E.A.—ENKI
"The Wise One"

*"I tell you, says Inanna-Ishtar,
that I am descending to the Underworld.
Father Enki, the Lord of Wisdom,
Who knows the secret of the Food of Life,
Who knows the Waters of Life,
He will surely listen; He will surely
bring me (back) to life."*
—Mardukite Tablet-C

Enki assisted his brother Enlil in developing the local universe, early Mesopotamian civilization, and organization of the physical world. As "Lord of the Earth" (ENKI) and "Dweller in Eridu" (E.A.), he is given a domain of knowledge and esoteric power related to magical and scientific wisdom. As Marduk's father, he is held in high regard in Babylonian tradition, revered as a protector of "younger generation" Anunnaki the one they all turn to as "Father," no matter their own lineage, when in the greatest need for wisdom or assistance.

Enki's city of Eridu marks the oldest city in Mesopotamia and the origins for what is called "Sumerian" civilization. As divine engineer and teacher of arts to humanity, he represents the archetypal wizard sage, the mentor of Marduk-the-Magician.

ESOTERIC CORRESPONDENCE.

Card Number : 9
Babylonian Anunnaki : E.A. ("The Deep One")
Sumerian Anunnaki : EN.KI ("Lord of Earth")
Mesopotamian Numerology : 40
Tarot Equivalent : The Hermit.
Kabbalistic : Mercy of Beauty.
Astrological : Jupiter acting through Virgo on the Sun.
Cosmic Domain : Sphere/Gate of Neptune.
Arts of Civilization (MEs) : Eldership, Wisdom, Counsel, Shepherding, Irrigation.
Keyword : The Wise Elder.

DIVINATION SYMBOLISM.

Description : E.A.—ENKI, the archetypal wise old Anunnaki wizard as famously depicted from the "*ad-da*" tablet, as residing in the remote (deep) of Eridu and shown with the flowing "waters of life."

Meaning : True wisdom and guidance (the responsibility of knowledge); true knowledge (answers available), hidden knowledge (scientific and energetic experiments), sharing knowledge (teaching), discretion (esoteric vs. exoteric knowledge), seclusion and external withdrawal (mind/awareness turned inward); self-knowledge and self-honesty.

Personality : The wise elder; the recluse or solitary loner.

Reversed : Socialization of information; community (exoteric knowledge), deceptions in knowledge relay (media communication); refusal to see truth (or acquire wisdom) and acceptance of propaganda; rejection of higher counsel (good advice) in preference of consensus.

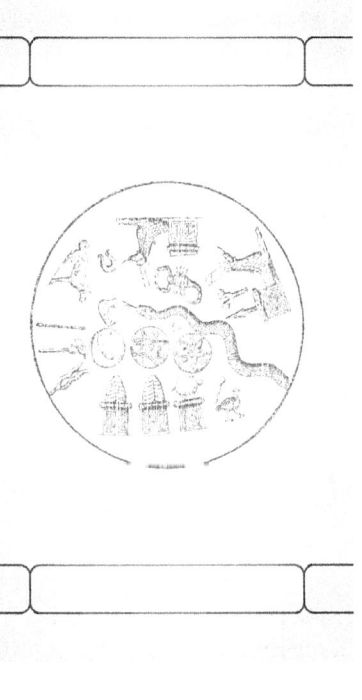

10. TABLET OF DESTINY
"Wheel of Fortune"

*"Tiamat exalted Kingu, raising him to power,
She gave him the Tablet of Destinies,
on his breast she laid them saying,
'Thy command shall not be in vain,
and your decrees shall be established.'"
"Then Marduk conquered Kingu,
and he rightly took the Tablets of Destiny.
He sealed them with his sign,
then hung them from his neck."*
—Mardukite Tablet-N

Although never recovered as a clay tablet artifact by archaeologists, numerous small mentions of *Tablets of Destiny* or a *Tablet of Destinies* appearing throughout Mesopotamian lore suggest that it offers supreme executive power of Cosmic Law. That it should be marked with an Elder Sign and later an insignia of its owner further suggests that it is also an entitlement record regarding cosmic authoritative command that is somehow universally recognizable.

ESOTERIC CORRESPONDENCE.

Card Number : 10
Babylonian Archetype : tup šīmātu or duppu šimat ("Tablet of Destinies")
Sumerian Archetype : dub.nam.tar.mes or dub namtarak ("Tablet of Destiny")
Mesopotamian Numerology : 2,160 (and 25920)
Tarot Equivalent : Wheel of Fortune.
Runic Symbolism : Raido
Ogham Symbolism : Reed ("nGetal")
Kabbalistic : Mercy of Victory
Astrological : Jupiter acting onto Venus.
Cosmic System (Domain) : The Eighth Sphere; Fixed Stars; Celestial Sphere.
Cosmic Law : Orderly Trend & Sequence. The Law of Fate & Destiny.
Arts of Civilization (MEs) : Astronomy and Astrology. Divination.
Keyword : Fate & Destiny.

DIVINATION SYMBOLISM.

Description : The wheel of the cosmos or celestial sphere (zodiac) of fixed star constellations or zones, each representing one of the Anunnaki pantheon, representing in full, a symbol of total cosmic order.

Meaning : Cosmic Law (orderly trend); consequential fate and destiny (by ordered sequence); the mere appearance of randomness (chance or fortune); observing causation (the order of things), natural law and karmic actions (succession); the ebb and flow of the tides of life (and transforming unplanned events); taking educated chances.

Personality : The gambler; the astrologer; a person who "plays the odds."

Reversed : Acceptance of randomness (disorder), inability to act (only react), the need to analyze and reevaluate all plans; dealing with unfortunate events or unexpected events (when things have "taken a turn").

11. ENLIL
"Justice"

"Enlil, whose command is far reaching;
Whose 'word' is lofty and holy;
Whose pronouncement is unchangeable;
Who decries destinies unto the distant future;
Gods of heaven and earth humble themselves
before the Lord of the Rightful Command..."
—The Sumerian Legacy

By the standards of the original system of Mesopotamia, Enlil is "Lord of Command," heir to "Anu-ship" in Heaven and the position of "God" for the local universe. For all "Enlilite" cultures, he was the god of the local space, the accessible god of the skies, representing Jupiter at the apex of a celestial pantheon before Marduk was elevated to this position in Babylon. As "God of the Airs," Enlil's domain constitutes the intermediary space bonding between the earth and heavens—and he is mainly the deity revered centrally in monotheistic Israelite (Hebrew), Christian and Islamic traditions.

Among the Anunnaki "younger pantheon" Enlil's heir was Ninurta (or Ninib) who was in wait for his place of Enlilship by way of the Old Tradition. Mardukite Babylonians systematically replaced Enlil with Marduk, and his heir, Ninurta-Ninib, became recognized as Guardian of the Saturn Gate—as religious, esoteric and mystical focus turns toward the supremacy of Enki's line.

ESOTERIC CORRESPONDENCE.

Card Number : 11
Babylonian Anunnaki : Il.Lil ("Lord of Airs")
Sumerian Anunnaki : En.Lil ("Lord of Airs")
Mesopotamian Numerology : 50
Tarot Equivalent : Justice
Runic Symbolism : Teiwaz
Ogham Symbolism : Ivy ("gort")
Kabbalistic : Strength (Severity) of Beauty.
Astrological : Mars acting through Libra on the Sun.
Cosmic Domain : Sphere of Jupiter.
Arts of Civilization (MEs) : el.ilu.tu (Enlilship), Agriculture, Adjustment/Equality.
Keyword : Command

DIVINATION SYMBOLISM.

Description : Enlil, Anunnaki god of the airs, stands in command of space, as shown on the *ad-da* tablet.

Meaning : Justice as a correcting balance (of equality); justice in fairness (consideration), justice as compensation (managing or adjusting all forces); harmony necessary for stability and order; fairness and honesty in decisions; the correct decision has been made.

Personality : A strong "fair" and balanced individual; a decision-maker.

Reversed : Injustice and (oppression) inequality, strong biases or prime dichotomy (taking sides), partial or incomplete decisions (not seeing the whole picture); bribery (influenced by persuasion), taking advantage ("tipping the scales").

12. MARDUK'S EXILE
"The Hanged Man"

"If I leave Babylon, says Marduk,
my legacy on earth will be destroyed.
If I leave Babylon,
If I leave my home in the E.Sag.Ila,
The Evil Winds, the Evil Demons,
The Evil Spirits of the Underworld,
They will rise up and devour the living;
All the creatures on the earth will they kill,
with none to turn them back."
—Mardukite Tablet-V

As soon as Babylonians elevated Marduk above all other "younger" Anunnaki—and without a consort from the Enlilite pantheon such as Inanna-Ishtar—the position and reign was ceaselessly attacked and undermined, causing schisms between Enki's offspring and Enlil's lineage. Marduk is removed (or exiled) from Babylon several times—even imprisoned for the mysterious death of Ishtar's lover, for whom she descends to the Underworld in search of.

Marduk's isolated exile and imprisonment represents standstills for a continuing legacy—times when plans are adjusted and developed although forced into retreat. In such instances, Marduk would become an "Unseen God" or Amon-Ra, and his legacy was upheld specifically by effots from his heir-son and herald. Nabu maintained a cabal order of cuneiform tablet scribe-priests that dedicated lifetimes to copying and circulating written records supporting the Mardukite legacy of Babylon.

ESOTERIC CORRESPONDENCE.

Card Number : 12
Babylonian Archetype : Marduk's Removal from Babylon.
Sumerian Archetype : Marduk's Exile (vs. Inanna-Ishtar); the Erra Epos.
Tarot Equivalent : The Hanged Man.
Runic Symbolism : Isa
Ogham Symbolism : Elder ("ruis")
Kabbalistic : Strength (Severity) of Glory.
Astrological : Mars acting through the water element onto Mercury.

Arts of Civilization (MEs) : Libel. Fallacy.
Keyword : Pause and Reflection.

DIVINATION SYMBOLISM.

Description : An obscure depiction of feudal wars between Inanna-Ishtar and Marduk before his exile (or imprisonment in the pyramids)—three pyramids and an *ankh* are visible at the bottom.

Meaning : Apparent standstill/stagnation (motion ceases), pause (activity halt), possible entrapment (unexpected decisions), passage of time (missed opportunity); withdrawal for introspection)

Personality : The "sacrificed" king.

Reversed : Arrogance (false security), poor planning, wasted time, indecision, imprisonment, false martyrdom, empty promises (false egotism), poor business (false contracts).

13. THE COSMIC TREE
"Tree of Life & Death"

"Lord Enki planted the Tree of Abzu in Eridu;
Its shade spreading over the Heavens—
Its grove spreading across the Earth."
—Mardukite Tablet-K

"And when Ningishzidda came forth,
He added two branches to the
Human (adamu) Tree of Life;
The tortuous serpent therein residing."
—Mardukite Tablet-G

The *Cosmic Tree*, "Flower," "seed" &tc. is the basic pattern of all energetic expression in the universe, representing microcosms and macrocosms on infinite scales. As an esoteric symbol, the "Tree of Life & Death" is often associated with DNA, else the "chain of genetic memory," and the fundamental singular origin of all forms and expressions interconnected as one. It is also the fundamental model by which "levels" and "layers" of manifestation are perceived, such as *"cabalistic"* examples.

As an oracular archetype, the Cosmic Law of Cyclicity is often only typified by death, which is but one transitional threshold of evolution. Secret societies even employ this archetype in elaborate initiation rites.

ESOTERIC CORRESPONDENCE.

Card Number : 13
Babylonian Archetype : Tree of Life and Gates of Death.
Sumerian Archetype : Gis.Zi.Da ("Tree of the Life Line"); Ki.Gal ("Great Lands" or "Great Underworld")
Mesopotamian Numerology : 8 or ∞
Tarot Equivalent : Death
Runic Symbolism : Eihwaz
Ogham Symbolism : Yew ("ioho")
Kabbalistic : Beauty of Victory.
Astrological : The Sun acting through Scorpio on Venus.
Cosmic System (Domain) : Law of Cyclicity.
Divine Decree (MEs) : Descent into (and ascent from) the Underworld.
Arts of Civilization (MEs) : Causation. Entropy.
Keyword : Cosmic Code.

DIVINATION SYMBOLISM.

Description : A famous depiction of the "cosmic tree" or "tree of life" from Mesopotamian art—the original cosmological pattern (kabbalah), based on the (date) palm tree.

Meaning : Transition (evolution and metamorphosis), death and rebirth (sudden change), renewal (new cycles on new/next level/phase); transformation (end of the old); loss/costs, unfortunate realization (cognitive dissonance), leaving the past behind to charge ahead.

Personality : The "dark" persona.

Reversed : Resistance to change (stalemate); deep turbulent changes (require completely new "goals"), shift in focus required; understanding bad situations (where one area lacks or stagnates, focus on another).

14. THE PATH (WAY)
"Ladder of Lights"

*"Marduk, surveyor of everything,
Who added to the people's knowledge
The power of Eternity-in-Infinity...
Marduk sets forth the way of walking
for the Seekers...
Choose your path and guide the people.
The compassionate eye of Marduk
Gazes on an erring race.
He shines upon the right way to go.
The Seeker is never forced on the path."*
—Mardukite Tablet-S

The "Serpent Path" is a tendency of movement across the "Tree of Life." This path has been clearly defined for us by many symbols and guideposts—but, the map is not the journey. A clear and straight path is not always evidently visible or apparent. One is forced to balance their movement in a progression that satisfies Cosmic Laws and will only reward or punish relative to the actual desires and aims of the Seeker.

The straightforward and direct pathway is always the preferred, but it is not popular or common—and few choose that course, preferring a natural inclination to test the extremes of polarity and boundaries of the system in a game of "walking the razor's edge." Validity of the path should be self-evident. Nothing is taken "on faith." All things become apparent in the end-game.

ESOTERIC CORRESPONDENCE.

Card Number : 14
Babylonian Archetype : E.zi.da (in Borsippa)
Sumerian Archetype : Ladder of Light
Mesopotamian Numerology : 7, 21, 22 and 120.
Tarot Equivalent : Temperance
Runic Symbolism : Dagaz
Ogham Symbolism : Blackthorn ("straif")
Kabbalistic : Beauty of Foundation.
Astrological : Sun acting through Sagittarius on the Moon.
Cosmic System : Virtue of Temperance,
Arts of Civilization (MEs) : Balance, Alchemic Science, Straightforwardness.
Keyword : Spiritual Evolution and Balance.

DIVINATION SYMBOLISM.

Description : The "serpent path" of action and movement.

Meaning : Set firmly on "the path"; channeling personal energy (balance between theoretical and practical); maintain current route (don't detour, but don't rush); patience (balancing time and progress); realistic expectations (results are contingent on what is "put in"); mixing/consuming elements to breakthrough new ones (alchemy).

Personality : A "level" person, but focused or determined.

Reversed : Unfocused energy (scattered attention), emotional stress (frustrations), toxic or volatile combinations; upset (discord), misalignment (the wrong path), competing with yourself ("out of phase").

15. TIAMAT
"The First Cause"

*"When in the heights the Heavens
had not been named,
And the Earth had not yet been named,
When no gods were yet called into being,
And the primeval Abzu (Abyss),
who birthed them, and Chaos,
Tiamat, the Ancient One,
Mother to them All,
Their waters were as One."*
—Mardukite Tablet-N

The opening lines from the Enuma Elis—or Babylonian Epic of Creation—given above, describes the absolute state of the cosmos, an ever-rolling abyss. It is Tiamat, the first cause and movement—often imagined as a primordial dragon—that represents All of Cosmic Law in motion, energetic activity, rippling across an infinite sea of Nothingness. In the Babylonian epic, Marduk slays the Cosmic Dragon, using her body to form the earth and her head to suspend heaven.

The Dragonslaying motif represents divinity and royalty in ancient lore—for the one who is master of the Cosmic Dragon is also seen as the master of Cosmic Law, the one who puts Order into Chaos. This force is also called *Kur* in Enlilite Sumerian literature, a word for "mountain," lending to the idea of world reign under the "King of the Mountain." Yet, some interpretations demonize this force as the responsible party in a physical "separation" from the "All."

ESOTERIC CORRESPONDENCE.

Card Number : 15
Babylonian Archetype : Tiamat
Sumerian Archetype : Usumgal ("The Cosmic Serpent"); Kur.
Mesopotamian Numerology : 600 (and 36000)
Tarot Equivalent : The Devil.
Runic Symbolism : Nauthiz
Ogham Symbolism : Pine ("pinne")
Kabbalistic : Beauty of Glory.
Astrological : The Sun acting through Capricorn onto Mercury.
Cosmic Domain : First Cause, Primum Mobile.

Arts of Civilization (MEs) : Cosmology.
Keyword : Primordial (Mother) Matrix.

DIVINATION SYMBOLISM.

Description : The "Cosmic Serpent" is seen encompassing a map of the cosmos as "First Cause"— The Law moving over the Infinity of Nothingness.

Meaning : Physical/material manifestation (the "First Cause"); material separation (worldly self-enslavement); physical/sensual indulgence, bondage to desires (obsession, selfishness, "materialism"); pride (arrogance), temptation (fall from grace); material control (egotism).

Personality : The materialist.

Reversed : Physical / material instability (chaos and lawlessness); over influence / external control (mind control and manipulation); greed and hoarding (material gain above all considerations).

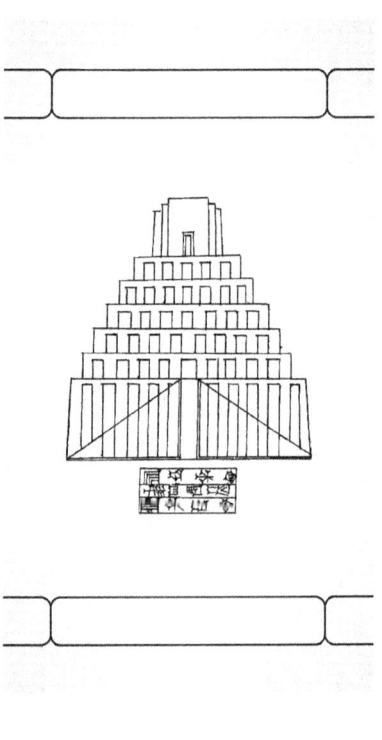

16. MARDUK'S TEMPLE
"The Tower of Babylon"

*"Again Marduk comes to build the
Foundation of Heaven-Earth,
A new temple to the heavens will be raised;
The Foundation of Heaven-Earth
will stand like a mountainside,
And the Gate of the Gods will be opened!"*
—Mardukite Tablet-R

A supreme ziggurat of Babylon was built and rebuilt several times in the course of Mesopotamian history. As with Marduk's exile or removal from Babylon, his tower was repeatedly razed, giving us our *Tower of Babel* archetype. A few Mardukite Kings, Hammurabi and Nebuchadnezzar II were dedicated to its reconstruction as a symbol of the Mardukite Babylonian legacy.

ESOTERIC CORRESPONDENCE.

Card Number : 16
Babylonian Archetype : E.Sag.Ila ("The Lofty

Temple-House of Marduk");
Bab.Ilu ("Babylon")
Sumerian (Archaic) Archetype : E.Temen.An.Ki
("Temple of Heaven on Earth");
Ka.Dingir.Ra.Ki ("Babylon") or
Tin.Tir.(a)(ki) ("Grove of Life")
Mesopotamian Numerology : 7, 18 and "3x60"
Tarot Equivalent : The (Falling) Tower.
Runic Symbolism : Fehu
Ogham Symbolism : Aspen ("eadha")
Kabbalistic : Victory of Glory (Splendor)
Astrological : Venus acting through Mars upon Mercury.
Cosmic System (Domain) : Spheres of Mars and Saturn.
Arts of Civilization (MEs) : Systematization, Reconstruction, Lamentation.
Divine Object (MEs) : The Exalted Shrine.
Divine Decree (MEs) : Destruction of Cities.
Keyword : Systematization; End of a Cycle and Beginning of another Cycle.

DIVINATION SYMBOLISM.

Description : The plans drawn for the "E.temen.an.ki" ziggurat of

Babylon (or "Tower of Babel") illustrated on an architectural builder's tablet rendering.

Meaning : Reconstructing, restructuring and remodeling (breakdown and release of the old to build anew); false hopes (if clinging to the old, unable to adapt); a severe and abrupt situational change (the "game has changed"); acceptance, reorganization and plan for (new opportunity) future; overcoming adversity against all odds.

Personality : A person with youthful power; a tenacious person.

Reversed : Inevitable change / breakdown (because "things fall apart"); the redundancy in life (clinging to the old, holding on too tightly to old ways); a need to see events and circumstances "as they really are"; inability to break away (brush off) traumatic events to see beneath.

17. INANNA-ISHTAR
"The Starry Goddess"

"Inanna-Ishtar, Queen of the Heavens,
Mistress of the Gods,
The Brightest Star in the Heavens.
She sought out the seven Divine Decrees
and grasped them in her hand.
With the garments of the Queen of Heaven
she dressed herself, and
With holy oils she anointed herself."
—Mardukite Tablet-C

Ishtar is the archetypal Venusian goddess of ancient Mesopotamia—the "Goddess of 10,000 Names"—also known as "Inanna" in Enlilite literature, or as Isis in Egypt. Elsewhere she is called Ashtoreth, Aphrodite or Astarte among many other titles. Her legacy is global in renown, and accessible to humans in the domains of love and war. Prowess and cunning earned her access to the Arts of Civilization, which she carried from *Eridu* to *Erech* (*Uruk*) to establish her place in the ancient Enlilite paradigm.

Originally equal and betrothed to Marduk as a power-couple, neither party wished to share supremacy, so Ishtar was given the Gate of Venus in Mardukite Babylon, and the primary goddess consort position to Marduk is then observed as Sarpanit for the "Lady (Queen) of Babylon."

ESOTERIC CORRESPONDENCE.

Card Number : 17
Babylonian Anunnaki : Ištar ("Ishtar")
Sumerian Anunnaki : Inanna or Anunitu
Mesopotamian Numerology : 15
Tarot Equivalent : The Star.
Runic Symbolism : Jera
Ogham Symbolism : Birch ("beith")
Kabbalistic : Victory of the Foundation.
Astrological : Venus acting through
    Aquarius on the Moon.
Cosmic Domain : Sphere/Gate of Venus,
    Virtue of Hope.
Arts of Civilization (MEs) : Divine Ladyship
Divine Decree (MEs) : Legacy of Divine
    Ordinance
Keyword : Hopes and Wishes.

DIVINATION SYMBOLISM.

Description : An antiquated depiction of the starry goddess of the heavens—Inanna-Ishtar—carrying sacred objects and seen above her totem in submission, the lioness.

Meaning : Accomplishment of goals and hopes (vital ambition in endeavors are fruitful), spiritual or divine assistance and guidance, renewed faith in self, personal fulfillment (feeling "blessed" or "favored" by the *gods*); situation is improving (more insight/clarity may be needed—illumination needed).

Personality : The "starry-eyed."

Reversed : False hopes (hopelessness), deception, pessimism (lack of self-confidence), self-doubt, poor judgment (choices/decisions are result of poor ideals); blurry or unsure ambitions (lack of clarity); stagnated from lack of ambition.

18. NANNA—SIN
"The Moon"

"Sin. Nannar. Mighty One among the gods.
Bright is thy light in the heavens,
Brilliant is thy torch, like the god-Fire,
Whose purpose no man learns,
The end of the month is thy day of oracle.
The thirtieth day is thy festival.
Namrasit, God of the New Moon,
In might unrivaled and
Whose purpose no man learns."
—The Sumerian Legacy

Ancient Mesopotamians likened the Moon to a "Sun at night," illuminating the path for long-range travelers or watching over the earth as it sleeps. Just as the Sun was a judge of daily actions, so too the domain of the moon governed the nightlife. The pre-Mardukite (Enlilite) lunar cult of Ur dedicated to the Moon god—Nanna—dominated a Sumerian religious consensus pertaining to the "younger" Anunnaki pantheon before the rise of Marduk's Babylon.

Nanna is the eldest son of Enlil though not an heir to Enlilship. Along with his consort named Ningal (or Nikkal) he maintains the lunar domain—and they are the parents to both Inanna-Ishtar (Venus) and Shammash (Sun), furthering the conception that light emerged forth from darkness (night) as is cosmologically demonstrated within the Enuma Elis regarding Abzu and Tiamat.

ESOTERIC CORRESPONDENCE.

Card Number : 18
Babylonian Anunnaki : Su.En / Sin ("Light of the Crescent Moon").
Sumerian Anunnaki : Nannar ("Light of the Full Moon"); As.Im.Babbar ("Light of the New Moon"); En.I.Zu.Na.
Mesopotamian Numerology : 30
Tarot Equivalent : The Moon
Runic Symbolism : Laguz
Ogham Symbolism : Willow ("saille")
Kabbalistic : Victory of the Kingdom
Astrological : Venus acting through Pisces on the Elemental (Material) Realm.
Cosmic Domain : Sphere/Gate of the Moon.

Arts of Civilization (MEs) : Mystery
Keyword : Shadows and Hidden Aspects.

DIVINATION SYMBOLISM.

Description : A famous royal depiction of the Anunnaki "elder god" Nanna seated on his throne by the light of the (crescent) moon.

Meaning : Unseen power (behind the scene) hidden (beneath the surface); unseen influences (subconscious, dreams, brainwashing, mind control); psychic development (use of intuition), self-reliance.

Personality : The "mysterious" one; a stranger.

Reversed : Deceptions and falsehoods, glamour and enchantment (things are not what they seem), hidden underlying influences (affecting thoughts and imagination), an undermining force, delusion (self-deception); emotion imbalance.

19. SHAMMASH (ŠAMAŠ)
"The Sun"

*"Šamaš, you are the light of everything,
You ceaselessly traverse the heavens,
Every day you pass over the broad earth.
Šamaš, your glare reaches down to the Abyss
and monsters of the deep behold your light.
Šamaš, the universe longs for your light.
What mountains do your rays not touch?
What region is not warmed by the
Brightness of your light?
Brightener of Gloom; Illuminator of Darkness;
You dispel the darkness
And illuminate the broad earth."*
—The Sumerian Legacy

The sun provides the brilliant and radiant power of sustainable life on earth. Praise and veneration of solar aspects was a celebration of life and order, acknowledging the physical presence and an ever watchful eye of the gods dispensing blessing and success to physical ventures of humans that live in accordance with Cosmic Law.

The Anunnaki role of sun-god carried the very name of the "face of the Sun" or Utu (Uddu), the "shinning one." The name of his consort, Aya (Aia) or Shendira, means "dawn." In these aspects, the divine couple represent the Stargate of the Sun—and in another capacity, Shammash is recognized as the Supreme Anunnaki Judge (*card 20*).

ESOTERIC CORRESPONDENCE.

Card Number : 19
Babylonian Anunnaki : Šamaš ("Shammash")
Sumerian Anunnaki : Uttu, Utu or Uddu.
Mesopotamian Numerology : 20
Tarot Equivalent : The Sun.
Runic Symbolism : Sowelu
Ogham Symbolism : Furze ("ohn")
Kabbalistic : Glory (Splendor) of the
    (Material) Kingdom.
Astrological : Mercury acting through the
    Sun onto the Moon.
Cosmic Domain : Sphere/Gate of the Sun,
Arts of Civilization (MEs) : Theology, Victory,
    "Rejoicing from the Heart"
Keyword : Victory.

DIVINATION SYMBOLISM.

Description : A famous depiction of the Anunnaki sun-god Šamaš shown on the "Hammurabi Law" stele.

Meaning : Brilliance and brightness (joy and happiness), success in worldly material cycles; growth, prosperity and fulfillment of personal wealth; business, new ventures, advancement, social success (friendship, engagements, offers, connections/networks); personal wholeness.

Personality : A successful charismatic type; Jovial types; also "show-offs."

Reversed : Misguided trust in others/social (networking); unstable finances and connections (investments); disagreements (that can lead to dishonesty and separation); need (require) more information before involving/investing yourself (time, money, energies, &tc.).

20. ANUNNAKI ASSEMBLY
"Council of the Watchers"
-or- "Šamaš as Judge"

*"By the command of Šamaš,
The Judge of Heavens and Earth,
May truth and righteousness
reign supreme throughout the lands.
By the decree of Šamaš, says Hammurabi,
I have been given my Eternal Legacy.
If a forthcoming ruler reads my words
and does not corrupt the law,
Then may Šamaš extend the length
of his reign on earth."*
—Mardukite Tablet-L

As a representative of heaven, the sun-god Šamaš symbolizes a physical presence and watchful "eye" of the gods. Šamaš is often invoked in Mesopotamian magic to bring righteous judgment to critical situations. As a fiery incinerator of iniquity, the sun purified or absolved the spirit—as illumination of darkness, Šamaš-the-judge revealed lies, and also truth, in all things.

In his capacity as "Chief" Anunnaki Judge of the Assembly, the solar domain includes law, truth and balance/restitution. As an oracular aspect, to "cut" a final judgment is to make an account and resolve the consequences of a completed cycle before that cycle or project is truly accomplished: the separation of the "net" from the "gross."

ESOTERIC CORRESPONDENCE.

Card Number : 20
Babylonian Anunnaki : Igigi ("Watchers");
    Anunnaki Judges/Guardians.
Sumerian Anunnaki : Shammash as Judge.
Mesopotamian Numerology : - - (or 180, 200)
Tarot Equivalent : Judgment
Runic Symbolism : Othila
Ogham Symbolism : Hawthorn ("huatha")
Kabbalistic : Glory of the Foundation.
Astrological : Mercury acting through Fire
    on the Spatial (Cosmic) Kingdom.
Cosmic System : Law of Compensation.
Divine Decree (MEs) : Truth (Highest Laws)
Arts of Civilization (MEs) : Judgment
Keyword : Restitution

DIVINATION SYMBOLISM.

Description : In a classic Sumerian depiction the god Shammash is seated at the front of an Anunnaki throne room overseeing the cosmic balance as humans come to face judgment.

Meaning : Accounting (settling accounts), the "final tally" (before the result is announced); nearing completion (final stages of a cycle); the "home stretch"; looking ahead (foresight); observation and guidance, trials and courts, laws and decrees.

Personality : The judge; the decider.

Reversed : Contemplation and reflection yields fears, guilt and regrets; the "mid-life" crisis or turning point; worries (of the unknown or death or change); all consequences require review before making future plans.

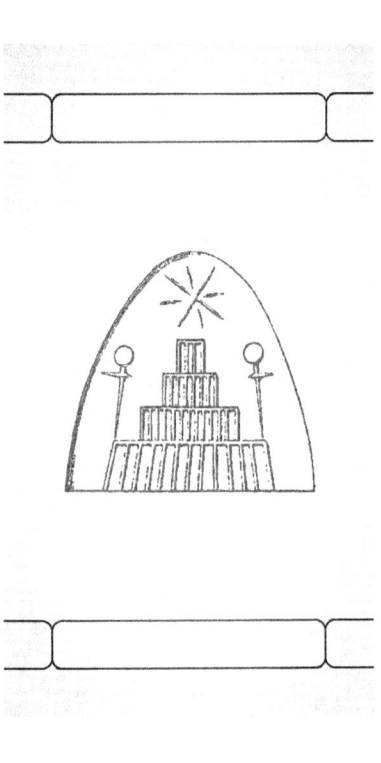

21. AN-KI
"The ALL"

*"From the knowledge of eternity-in-infinity,
I draw a circle with my stylus on the tablet.
Everything is in that world,
which also applies to this one—
and there are still a thousand times more.
The circle marked shows nothing more
than a small image of the Great All.
How is one thing different from another?
How is the circle at the beginning
different then at the end of this.
They are the beginning and the end;
one as is the other.
Whatever you start in the earth world
is not separate;
it significantly and necessarily has its
higher counterpart in the Otherworld.
The circle has neither beginning or end,
and yet we behold its existence.
So it is with the great cycle of
eternity-in-infinity;
Eternally connected is All-as-One"*
—Mardukite Tablet-S

In most basic terms, an early cuneiform term to denote the "cosmos" or an "All-as-One" existence combines the ideograms of "sky/heaven" (AN) and "earth" (KI) as the word ANKI or "Universe" of all that is seen and unseen—all that is below and above.

ESOTERIC CORRESPONDENCE.

Card Number : 21
Mesopotamian Archetype : An.Ki ("Heaven" + "Earth" or "all existence")
Mesopotamian Numerology : 3,600 and 216,000
Tarot Equivalent : The Universe.
Runic Symbolism : Hagalz
Ogham Symbolism : Ash ("nuin")
Kabbalistic : Foundation of the Kingdom.
Astrological : The Cosmos.
Cosmic System (Domain) : Cosmic Existence.
Arts of Civilization (MEs) : All-as-One.
Keyword : Totality and Completion.

DIVINATION SYMBOLISM.

Description : The "completed temple"—the

"bond" or "foundation" of heaven and earth, meaning the whole universe—the realization of all in mystic unity.

Meaning : Finality, successful completion of the journey or major cycle (the temple build is complete); all is in perfection (according to plan); freedom and renewal (a sense of true accomplishment or feeling of a "job well done"); a higher state or evolution (cycle) beginning; new higher ideals; the deserved successful hard-fought victory.

Personality : The ascended master.

Reversed : An incomplete cycle/project/goal (incompetence or frustration); refusal to "think outside the box" or explore "new horizons" (to succeed); rigidity, stubbornness and resistance to changing conditions leads to failure.

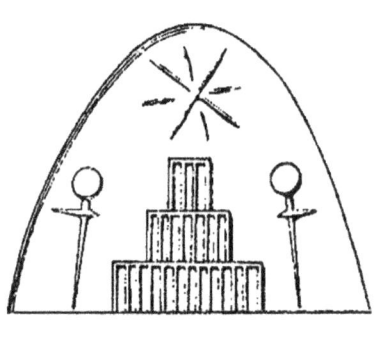

THE ORACLE

CONSULTING THE ORACLE
"Reading the Cards"

There are no absolute standards or rules for working with an oracle—all traditional symbolism and practices are the result of observations and experimentation spanning hundreds, if not thousands, of years. This being said: there is a general trend or consensus among classic teachings of mystics and magicians that lends us hints and clues toward developing a more personal approach as one grows with experience in using this type of "cartomancy" (or card symbol divination).

A preliminary familiarity with the actual cards (and imagery) offers greater success of using their oracular value. The same is true concerning their mythic and historic backgrounds within the specifically Babylonian "Mardukite" worldview (paradigm) —all of which is concisely described on the previous pages of this book, of which may also be supplemented with other material.

As a personal tool—or sacred tool—oracles are always treated with respect and often are kept away from "casual" view or the arbitrary handling from others. Many who use tarot cards and other such devices today will often keep their "pack" or deck wrapped in a dark material, often black, as a physical and energetic shelter. This also maintains an aura that they are not everyday common place items—that they are sacred. They should, however, carry your own personal individual "charge." This is accomplished naturally by your handling of them and use in meditations.

When used as an oracular device, the tarot cards are shuffled and "cut" based on the intuition of the practitioner. They may also be "fanned." When they are read for others, some will allow that person to perform this step; others are more particular, either allowing no one else to handle their tools at all—or else, only allowing another person to touch them when a card is to be selected from the fanned pack, or when the deck is to be cut.

Diviners and seers using oracular devices will develop their own unique methods of practice. Personal standards become "ritualized" over time with repeated use and familiarity—forming a *tradition*. They are so numerous in fact, that entire books are dedicated to little else. Various theories also exist correlating cartomancy phases to left-right brain activity where it is suggested to use this-or-that hand for cutting or laying out cards, &tc. Likewise, some diviners utilize reversed meanings in their interpretation, returning to the deck any fallen cards during shuffles in the same manner they fell.

In addition to games and fortune-telling, tarot cards are also mnemonic devices for key archetypes and esoteric lessons, much like the *Nordic Runes* or *Druidic Ogham*. Use of a preselected "significator" card in the readings materializes this. It is placed beneath of, or substitutes, the card that best represents the basis of the question/need or general state of the *querent* or "Seeker"; e.g. *lovers* for love, *chariot* for travel, &tc.

The arts of divination and oracular use is something that can only be described in a "how-to" book such as this, which mainly emphasizes the unique Anunnaki elements into an already well-established method. A preexisting background in esoteric arts of concentration and meditation, or previous use of divinatory systems, is not required, but may be beneficial. For those coming upon this lore "early" on their path: the methodology presented within this book and card set is more than adequate to base an ongoing developmental pursuit.

It is important to note—contrary to how many others may present similar oracles—that this current "system" is a *tool* for personal exploration and spiritual growth or evolution. It draws from the most ancient archetypal symbolism and iconography on the planet to display a complete "method" of gaining *insights* from ritual, meditation or divination that is consistent with roots of its ancient symbolism and the modern "New Age" methods of practice. It is *only* a tool or catalyst—the *real* power being: you.

The basic premise behind *cartomancy* is simple: There is a series of variable cards or symbols, each carrying a specific theme or array of key meanings; there is a series of variable determinations or positions a possible card or symbol may occupy; and finally, someone—observer or interpreter—must make a correlation between placement of symbols and the situational query.

Whereas the symbolism of the archetypes or cards has been given previously, the following section describes manners that the cards may be laid out—called a *layout* or *spread*. These "spreads" are specifically designed to compliment Anunnaki themes of Babylonian tradition, but they are only suggestions. Any similar type of layout can be substituted for personal preference.

There is one final main point of discussion before turning you loose on the oracle—a matter of the degree or level of cultural or ceremonial (ritual) intricacy incorporated into the practice of divination. This, again, is subject to personal preference, but will be important for some of our readers here.

The act of consulting an oracle is a spiritual exercise in meditation that is treated as formal or casual as the seer requires. Some people have treated "tarot" cards as little more than a game—whereas others have used its symbolism as a tool for personal exploration, growth and development—or as an aid to outlining and planning personal endeavors. It is important that any oracle remain a personal clarifying tool, not as a replacement or substitute for using good judgment; a perfecting catalyst, not a crutch to carry the weight.

In ancient times, powers of the oracle are exercised by a "seer"—a specialized priest or priestess of the temple. A sacred space would already exist within the temple for this operation, but a modern practitioner can easily designate space, appropriating an altar and carpet within a defined circle. Boundaries of the circle may be marked by a line of consecrated "Flour of Nabu"—also called the "Flour of Nisaba" on some older tablets. The area may be decorated to personal taste, if none of it is distracting.

Basic instructions for ceremonial formulae may be derived from Mardukite Tablet-B, where it states:—always observe the pious ways and the Rites of Offering at the Altar of Sacrifice before an image of your god and goddess. Intone prayers from the tablets and make sweet offerings of incense, grain, honey, butter and libations of wine and milk. Bowls of anointing oils and water are placed before the deities, as well as offerings of lapis lazuli, gold and alabaster.

An altar cloth or "spread cloth" may be on the altar—a piece of cloth material used only to lay out the cards on. Some people use this to wrap up their cards between "readings."

A prayer or invocation may facilitate initial energetic movement or exchange, else "communication." This projects or speaks intentions of the seer, followed by the act of "meditation," which is a reception of information—the part where a seer must be able to hear, listen or receive the answers sought; contemplating and understanding what is given.

DIVINATION & MEDITATION
"The Card Spreads"
— —

•BABILI•
   "The Gates of Babylon"
      (The Initiate's *3-card spread*)

•ETEMENANKI•
   "The Tower of Babylon"
      (The Builder's *6-card spread*)

•ESAGILA•
   "The Temple of Marduk"
      (The Diviner-Priest's *6-card spread*)

•ANUNNA•
   "The Anunnaki Assembly"
      (The Priest-King's *8-card spread*)

•ISTARI•
   "The Anunnaki Star"
      (The God's *10-card spread*)

— BABILI —
The Gates of Babylon
"The Initiate's 3-Card Spread"

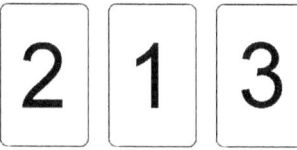

Gates and Walls of Babylon are constructed from a sequence of supportive bricks connected to one another in series. The basic *Babili Spread* is used to determine the current "position"/"state" of an "initiate" or *querent*—the one seeking knowledge—in addition to most critical or relevant influences, forces or energies affecting this—both those carried from the past affecting future results, and also future influences.

1.) Present state or position; where the energy is; the "consciousness."
2.) Past influences; where the energy was; the "substance."
3.) Future expectations; where energy will be; the "motion" or activity.

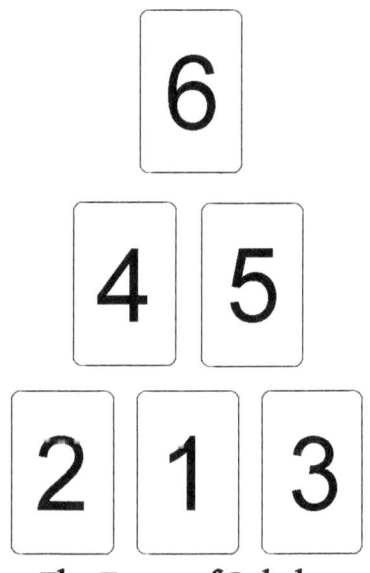

The Tower of Babylon

— ETEMENANKI —
The Tower of Babylon
"The Builder's 6-Card Spread"

As with the Gates and Walls of Babylon, an interconnected sequence of clay bricks are used to build the famous ziggurat pyramid of Babylon—the *E.Temen.An.Ki* or "Tower of Babel." Obviously many more bricks are required to build a tower than a section of wall or gate—and obviously the integrity of the relationship between the bricks and building levels are even more critical if the tower is to stand—and goals are to be accomplished. As such, the *E.Temen.An.Ki Spread* is most useful for inquiries regarding specific plans, projects and goals.

The foundation cards (1-3) represent those factors closest to you, other immediate influences and your own efforts. The middle tier (4-5) concerns visible developments and outside or emerging external factors. The final outcome (6) is demonstrated by the apex display of the tower.

TOWER OF BABYLON 6-CARD SPREAD

1.) The original state, position, plans or starting point; "consciousness."
2.) The past or supportive influences and experiences to draw from; "substance."
3.) The future or required movement/direction of resource to establish firm foundations; "action."
4.) The view from the outside; external opinions, feelings or assistance; influence from other people.
5.) The view from the inside; what is necessary to complete the project; or else, how to present yourself.
6.) The final state or project condition based on the current supporting or contributory influential aspects.

— ESAGILA —
The Temple of Marduk
"The Diviner-Priest's 6-Card Spread"

The *Temple of Marduk Spread* uses a similar form-shape from the *E.Temen.An.Ki Spread*, except in this instance, the Temple Tower is already built and ready for the priests and priestesses—"diviners" utilizing the completed temple to approach the deity (Marduk, &tc.) and "divine" or call down messages and answers. While a "builder" is concerned with a specific goal or set of plans, this *Temple of Marduk Spread* is more appropriate for general queries and more abstract questions—such as those brought to the temple in ancient times.

TEMPLE OF MARDUK 6-CARD SPREAD

1.) The *querent* or question itself; overall focus or main aspect of what is presented to the temple; alternately a preselected "significator" card representing the same.

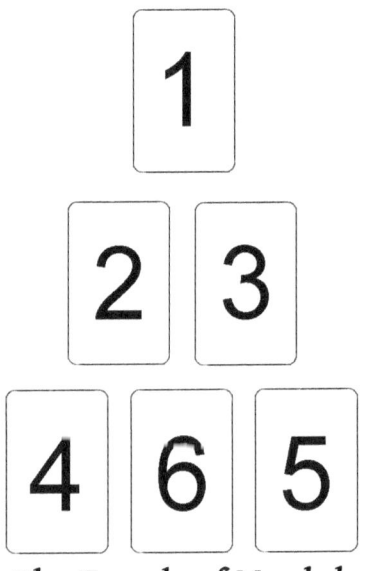

The Temple of Marduk

2.) External challenges, obstacles or oppositions; external factors or complications requiring handling or full resolution to move forward.
3.) Internal challenges set up by the *querent*, real or imagined; fears and expectations requiring resolution.
4.) The supplication for support; the foundations to establish resolution and a successful goal, including outside assistance, past experience or inner abilities that are required.
5.) The surrounding factors; external influences contributing to the final outcome; or else, variables that may directly alter the outcome.
6.) General answer or potential outcome based on the currently displayed movement of energy and resources (shown by the surrounding cards).

— ANUNNA —
The Anunnaki Assembly
"The Priest-King's 8-Card Spread"

The *Great Assembly* or *Council of Anunnaki* could be depicted in a multiplicity of ways, but we have chose an example called by some scholars: the *Seven Anunnaki Judges*—or else, the *Seven Anunnaki Gate-Guardians* of the "Mardukite" Babylonian pantheon. These seven figures simultaneously represent the seven levels of the supreme ziggurat, the seven planets and seven rays or energy currents esoterically equated or systematized as the seven notes of music, seven colors of the visible spectrum, seven "chakras" of the personal human energy system, and so forth.

The seven primary aspects (1-7) each relate to a wide-angle relationship with the entire cosmos, including the progression of spiritual evolution or "ascension" along the "Ladder of Lights"—of which ancient initiates experienced as seven stages or

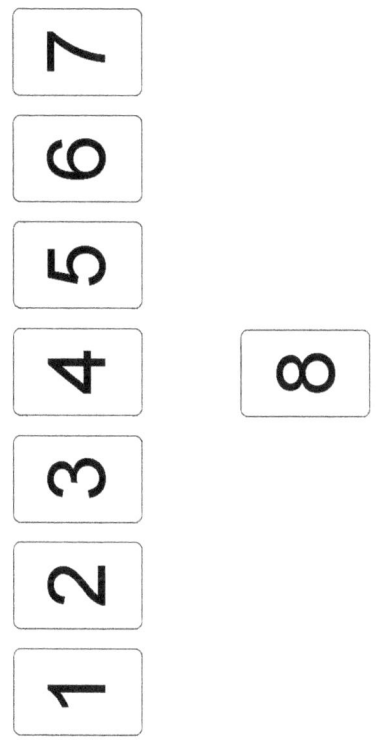

The Anunnaki Assembly

seven states of the human condition. The eighth card (8) represents the state, status or position of the *querent* or initiate (Truth Seeker). Standing before the Assembly of Anunnaki, this card may be preselected as the "significator."

Each position within the Grand Assembly is held by a specific Anunnaki deity, with specific "advice" or information correlating to that which is within their domain. Descriptions for interpreting the seven (7) are based on the same sequence described of the "Temple of the Seven Spheres" or E.ZIDA—home of the "Oracle of Nabu" in Borsippa and mirrored in the structure of Babylon's famous ziggurat.

ANUNNAKI ASSEMBLY CARD SPREAD

1) Sphere of the Moon—Seat of Nanna
    Domain of dreams, enchantment, magical/psychic development.
2) Sphere of Mercury—Seat of Nabu
    Domain of communication, mental development, knowledge, learning.

3) Sphere of Venus—Seat of Ishtar
    Domain of beauty, love, fertility, social, emotional development.
4) Sphere of the Sun—Seat of Shammash
    Domain of leadership, authority, material development and wealth.
5) Sphere of Mars—Seat of Erra-Nergal
    Domain of war, destruction, self-annihilation and purification.
6.) Sphere of Jupiter—Seat of Marduk
    Domain of business and expansion, the "legacy" and longevity.
7.) Sphere of Saturn—Seat of Ninurta
    Domain of dark, hidden influences; the shadow self or alter-ego.

— ISTARI —
The Anunnaki Star
"The God's 10-Card Spread"

The original ancient *Anunnaki Star*-sign—origins for the modern asterisk—is derived from an eight-pointed cuneiform sign that scribes used to designate the "heavens," "sky gods," "stars," "planets" and other celestial objects. This supreme sign ("AN") also represents *all* that is not earth, material or physical—meaning, for our purpose, the full body of knowledge and wisdom of the cosmos, called "Cosmic Law" to some and realized or represented by an astral "Akashic Library" to others.

As a model of card divination, the design for interpreting the *Anunnaki Star Spread*, also called "*Anunnaki Cross*" or "*Babylonian Cross*," corresponds exactly to positions of the most multipurpose and widely used of all tarot spreads, the "*Celtic Cross Spread*," interpreted here based on Joshua Free's "*Arcanum: Great Magical Arcanum.*"

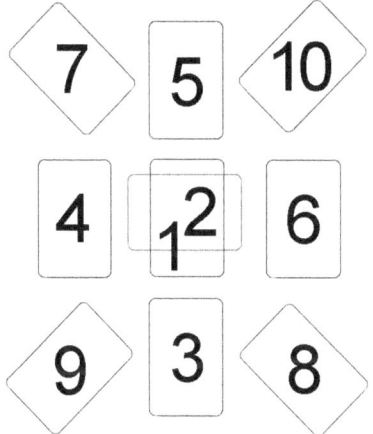

The Anunnaki Star

1.) "This envelops you" – representing the observer or *querent* of the question; the general atmosphere, aura or personal (inner) influence affecting the current position or state; alternately a "significator."
2.) "This crosses you" – representing immediate obstacles, opposition or challenges (blocks, barriers, &tc.) to overall success.
3.) "This is beneath you" – representing basic foundations already evident (in play) or manifested, which may be drawn from as resource, proof or experience.
4.) "This is behind you" – representing the immediate background, what has passed or is passing away, ending or leaving the situation.
5.) "This crowns you" – representing overt aims or ideals of the *querent*, what is still potential or not yet actualized and may be encouraged or avoided (as it applies).
6.) "This is before you" – representing upcoming inflowing energies or

influences taking shape or forthcoming in the near future based on past and present influences.

7.) "This is your persona" – representing (together with the third card) your persona, the true and underlying attitudes and beliefs that will become evident or expressed, or reflecting how to project/carry yourself to others concerned.

8.) "This is your house" – representing how and what others perceive, their beliefs and opinions and generally the external sources of influence projected onto the situation or environment.

9.) "This is your hopes and fears" – representing true feelings, hidden aspects or thoughts of the *querent* or observer, including inhibitions and reservations, real or imagined, that affect the outcome.

10.) "This is the outcome" – representing the final result or answer based on the current energy progression illustrated by surrounding cards.

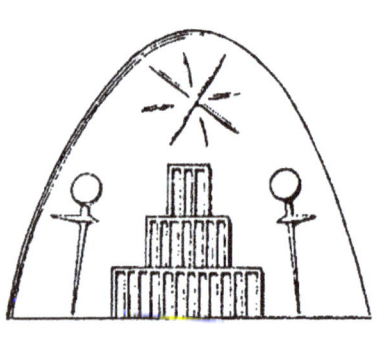

APPENDIX

— APPENDIX —
The Anunnaki Tarot
"Paper Card Deck Set"

This book was originally prepared to companion a physical card deck developed and distributed by the Mardukite Research Organization and available separately. In the meantime, we chose to reproduce the card images as an appendix for this title in such a way that they may be effectively cut out and used without affecting the remainder of the book. Should you choose to remove the rear pages to do this, the shape of the book may be maintained by attaching an appropriate sized envelope or plastic bag to the inside back cover that can hold your paper deck of cards when not being used, filling page space to maintain the binding. Alternately the rear pages may be used for meditation or coloring purpose. The card titles are blank in this book so that a seer may insert the most applicable keyword to their level of experience—whether a traditional title or Anunnaki motif, &tc.

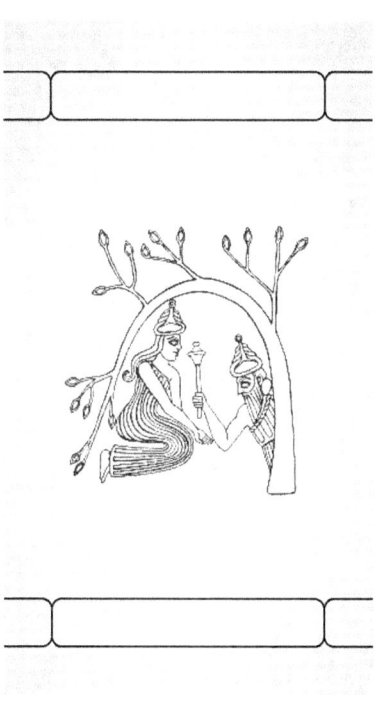

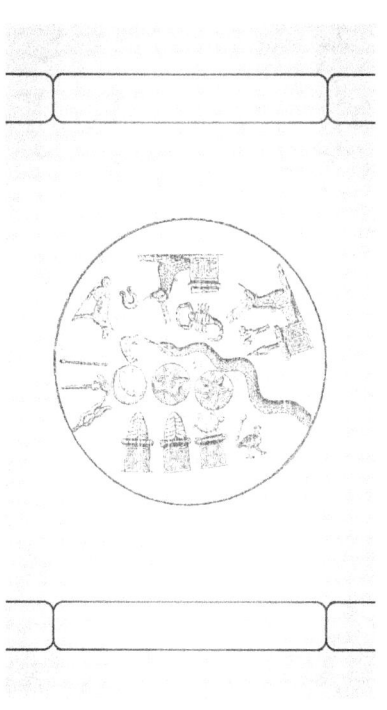

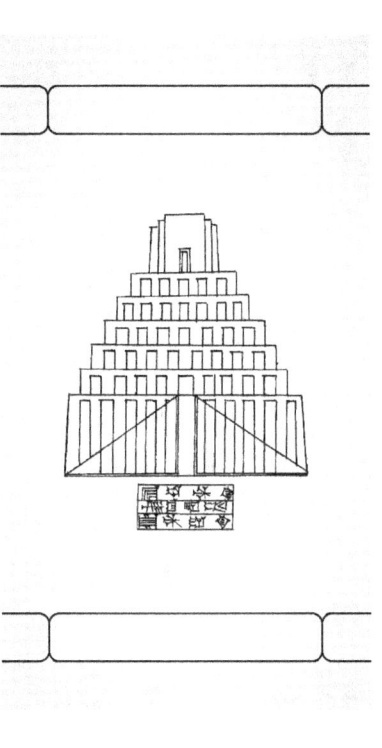

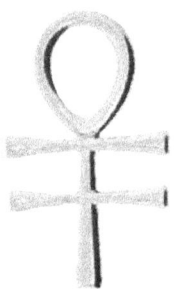

PUBLISHED BY THE **JOSHUA FREE** IMPRINT REPRESENTING

Mardukite Truth Seeker Press — **mardukite.com**

[Mardukite Liber-T]

www.ingramcontent.com/pod-product-compliance
Lightning Source LLC
Chambersburg PA
CBHW071359290426
44108CB00014B/1618